100 COLOUR PHOTOGRAPHS

VENICE

HEART OF THE WORLD

BONECHI EDITORE

Firenze – Via dei Rustici, 5

Concessionario per Venezia
ROBERTO BENEDETTI

VENICE

ARRIVING AT VENICE. - One can get to Venice by sea, by car or by train. Here we are at the car station in **Piazzale Roma** which one reaches by passing over the new Ponte della Libertà constructed alongside the railway in 1933. The great garage is also the departure point for the motor coaches that link the city with its sister cities on the mainland. At the **Fondamenta di S. Croce** one gets aboard the steamboat that takes one to St. Mark's Square along the Grand Canal; it takes a good thirty minutes of navigation to complete the trip.

THE GRAND CANAL

Here is a wide view of a tract of the Grand Canal. This stupendous artery with its sparkling surface, seen from above, assumes the shape of an « S » back to front which divides the city in half. It is 3.800 metres long, its width varies between thirty and seventy metres and it is 5 metres deep.

In order to enjoy the whole of the Grand Canal it is necessary to travel along it in a gondola because this is the only means of transport from which one can really admire the particular splendour of the small canals, palaces, large squares, canals and foundations, any one of which proposing a real motive of beauty which is always present at whatever time of the year.

For people of culture every glance brings back a historical, artistic or literary memory, whereas simpler people feel an unrepeatable suggestion and commotion that really shouts at them from the incomparable scene that is placed before them; a changeable landscape that benefits from sun and clouds, from rain and the impetuosity of the sea, and from the vegetation and the multiform sequence of houses and palaces, giving it an unreal and suggestive atmosphere that no other city in the world is able to express.

Right after coming out of the station, on the other side of the Grand Canal is the church of **San Simeone and Giuda,** known as San Simeone Piccolo, which really commands the respect of all tourists with its dainty copper dome in a vivid green colour. It was founded in the IX century, but the present construction was realised between 1718 and 1738 inspired by the Roman Pantheon. The architect was Giovanni Scalfurotto and the interior is built on a circular plan.

This is the very beautiful church of **Santa Maria di Nazareth,** called **of the Scalzi,** erected between 1660 and 1689 on a design by Baldassarre Longhena. Its rich facade is the work of Giuseppe Sardi, a singular example of Venetian baroque style inspired by classical forms. The tomb of the last Doge of Venice Lodovico Manin is kept in its interior.

7

The picturesque church of **San Geremia** which was built in the XI century but reconstructed in the XIII century. Here the body of the Siracusan martyr Santa Lucia is kept. The high Romanesque bell tower is one of the most ancient in Venice; at its side is Palazzo Labia covered with scaffolding for restoration, and on the left is the seventeenth century Palazzo Flangini, the work of the architect Giuseppe Sardi.

The Fondaco dei Turchi (the Warehouse ▶ of the Turks), so-called because it was the seat of merchants from the Orient in the past. The construction, which is in Venetian-Byzantine style of the XIII century, presents architectural reminiscences of the Ducal Palace. Inside it contains the Civic Museum of Natural History.

CA' PESARO. - It is a powerful and magnificent Venetian palace in baroque style, the masterpiece of the architect Baldassarre Longhena (1679-1710). It contains the International Gallery of Modern Art and the Collection of Oriental Art.

THE CA' D'ORO is in magnificent Venetian style of the fifteenth century, and its name is derived from the gilding that decorated its facade in the past. It is the work of Bartolomeo Bon and Matteo Raverti (1421-40) and was ordered from them by the patrician Marin Contarini. When the palace came into the propriety of Baron Giorgio Franchetti, he gave it to the State in 1916 including the collection of art that carries his name.

The Fabbriche Nuove di Rialto (the New Rialto Buildings), are a lesser work by Jacopo Tatti known as Sansovino (1555), now the seat of the Tribunal.

The Fabbriche Vecchie di Rialto (the Old Rialto Buildings), were built in the first half of the sixteenth century, the work of the architect A. Abbondi usually called Scarpagnino. The fruit and vegetable market is held here.

(above) On the right is the **Fondaco dei Tedeschi** (the Warehouse of the Germans), so-called because the German merchants gathered here in order to trade their manufactures and to buy the goods coming from the East. The architecture is by Scarpagnino (1508). The Central Post Office stands here. After the Rio del Fondaco are other characteristic palaces which repeat Venetian styles. (below) **The Rialto Bridge**.

CA' FOSCARI. - It is the most beautiful example of Venetian Gothic architecture. It is owed to the initiative of Doge Francesco Foscari who directed the political and social life of the life of the Republic for more than thirty years. The receptions he gave were famous, especially the one in 1574 when King Henry II of France stayed here. Nowadays it is the seat of the University Institute of Economy and Commerce. ▶

Ca' Rezzonico and the **Academy Bridge.** - This palace of the seventeenth century is very beautiful in baroque style and built by the architect Baldassarre Longhena. The top floor is an eighteenth century addition by Giorgio Massari. The Academy Bridge, all in wood (1932) is in one arch and leads to the Academy Gallery, the main museum of the city which contains masterpieces of Venetian painting.

PALAZZO GRASSI. - This powerful construction in the classical style of the XVIII century is owed to Giuseppe Massari. The Grassi family, originally from Bologna, were enscribed in the patrician order in 1718. The palace is now the seat of the International Centre of Arts and Customs. ▶

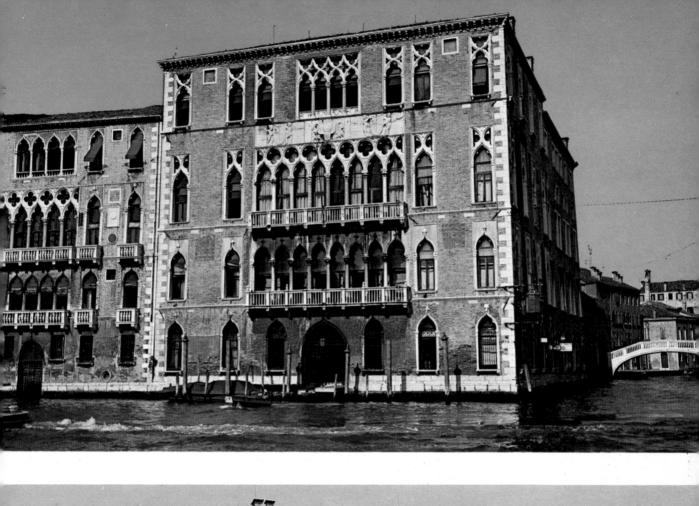

Palazzo Cavalli Franchetti is one of the most beautiful examples of Gothic architecture of the fifteenth century. One notes the decoration of the facade which brings the covered loggia of the Ducal Palace into mind.

SANTA MARIA DELLA SALUTE. - Close by St. Mark's Square on the right of the Great Canal and greatly admired by visitors to the city is the very lovely church of **Santa Maria della Salute,** a masterpiece in baroque style by the architect Baldassarre Longhena. The building on an octagonal design and surmounted by a dome was built following a decree by the Venetian Senate on October 22nd 1630 to thank the Virgin Mary for the end of the plague that had taken 47 thousand victims. The magnificent and powerful white mass has impressed the sensibility of painters of all times who have immortalised it on their canvases and in their etchings.

ST. MARK'S SQUARE

This is the stupendous and enormous open-air hall of the Venetians. Here the political, social and religious life of the city was unrolled and continues to do so even today, and here the echo of all the great happenings of which the glorious Republic was a protagonist is synthetised in a harmonious frame. The great square in trapezoidal form is 175 and a half metres long, 82 metres wide at the basilica end and 57 metres wide at the opposite end. The arrangement of the paving in Euganean trachyte and white strips is the work of the architect Andrea Tirali who carried it out in 1723. In ancient times the surface of the square was called « Morso » because of the nature of the ground which was firmer than anywhere else, indeed so much so that a canal flowed here and it was surrounded by trees.

St. Mark's Square: (above) on the left is the **Procuratie Nuove** (the residence of the Attorneys of St. Mark) the classical work of Vincenzo Scamozzi (1584); in the blackground is the **Napoleonic wing** in neoclassical style by the architect Giuseppe Soli (1807). (Below) The **Procuratie Vecchie** built between 1400 and 1500 perhaps from a design by Mauro Codussi.

THE CLOCK TOWER. - Here is a view of the terminal part with the belfry and the two « Mori » (Moors), so-called for the darkened patina that the bronze has assumed, who have struck the hours for more than four centuries. In fact they were cast in bronze by Ambrogio de le Anchore in 1497. Next to them on the same tower is the **winged Lion,** the emblem of Venice and below the **Virgin and Child** in gilded beaten copper, the fifteenth century work of the sculptor and goldsmith Alessandro Leopardi. In front of the Madonna is a little golden terrace where during Ascension week the Magi Kings preceded by an angel pass bowing in front of the Virgin.

A beautiful picture of the Clock Tower constructed by Mauro Codussi between 1496 and 1499.

The thick **flight of the doves in St. Mark's Square** wishing a welcome to tourists from all over the world. An ancient legend says that the doves were brought to Venice from the Island of Cyprus in homage to the wife of the Doge. Anyway they are considered a really traditional ornament to the square, so much so that the Commune occupies itself with keeping them, distributing an abundant ration of maize to them twice a day.

THE BELL TOWER OF ST. MARK. - Framed between the Sansovino Library and the corner of the Ducal Palace can be seen the **bell tower of St. Mark** identical to the ancient one that collapsed on July 14th 1902 and which was built on Roman foundations between 888 and 912. The new bell tower, the « paron de casa » (master of the house) as the Venetians call it, was inaugurated in 1912 for the feast day of St. Mark the protector of the city. It is ´98,60 metres high and one can enjoy a wonderful view of Venice and the Lagoon from the belfry cell. A gilded angel swings on the cusp according to the direction of the wind.

THE BASILICA OF ST. MARK

It has been defined and it is the monument that selfcontains all the political, social and religious history of the Republic. Its origins are very ancient, it stood in 829 in the time of the Doge Giustiniano Partecipazio who had it built to hold the remains of the Evangelist St. Mark who became the one patron of the city. In 927 the basilica was destroyed by fire and rebuilt in the same architectural forms that it has today by Doge Domenico Contarini between 1043 and 1071.

The building keeps to the plans of the Byzantine churches, constructed on a Greek plan with domes, but interpreted in a Romanesque way. The primitive and solemn nudity of the church was soon forgotten when the very beautiful mosaic decoration was carried out, with precious marbles and architectural elements that came from the Orient with the result that Byzantine, Gothic, Islamic and Renaissance style are present in it. In this way the great golden basilica became a complex masterpiece of art thanks to the talent of famous artists and very clever Venetian workmen.

The scenographic view of the **principal facade** which measures 51,80 metres in height. The five entrance doors in Romanesque style with oblique arching towards the interior have their logical completion in the great arches above which are nobly interrupted by a subtle balustrade animated by the leaping horses and subdued by the spires and domes in fascinating eastern taste. The whole of the facade is made more precious by rich marble decoration and splendid mosaics in the portals and great arches. The three bronze pillars in front of the Basilica where the gonfalons of the Republic were hoisted in the past, are the valuable works by the sculptor and goldsmith Alessandro Leopardi who carried them out in 1505.

« The transport of the body of St. Mark »
mosaic of 1260-70.

« The Venetians pay homage to the body of
St. Mark » by L. Ricci, 1728.

THE MOSAICS IN THE LUNETTES ABOVE THE ENTRANCE DOORS

« The arrival at Venice of the body of St.
Mark » by P. Vecchia, 1660.

« The carrying off of the body of St. Mark
from Alexandria in Egypt » by P. Vecchia, 1660.

The Main Portal of the facade with the « Judgement of the World » by L. Querena, 1836. ▶

The Deposition of Christ.

The Descent into Hell.

THE MOSAICS OF THE SPIRES. - These were carried out by A. Gaetano, from cartoons by Maffeo da Verona, between 1617 and 1618.

The Resurrection of Christ.

The Ascension of Christ.

The great central spire of the facade is a masterpiece of Tuscan sculptoral art. The Evangelist St. Mark and the angels who climb up towards him are the work of the Florentine Niccolò Lamberti who carried them out at the beginning of 1400.

One can admire the **Four Horses** in gilded copper which came from Constantinople as spoils of war to the Doge Enrico Dandolo during the Fourth Crusade in 1204 against the great central window of the upper facade. The quadriga was placed here in around the middle of the fourteenth century, then it tempted Napoleon so that he took it to Paris on the 17th December 1707 from where it returned to Venice in 1815.

THE INTERIOR OF THE BASILICA OF ST. MARK. - The sumptuous interior of the Basilica which has conserved its Byzantine architectural structure given it at the time of Doge Contarini is on a central plan in a Greek cross with a main nave, a raised presbytery and at the arms of the cross the minor naves pass, divided by pilasters and columns that support the matron's gallery. Pointed arches, resting on corner pillars, are the solid support for the five domes.

Originally the walls and pilasters had no marble covering, this was started in 1159 using precious and varied materials which came for the most part from civil and religious buildings in the East and Dalmatia. The splendid mosaic decoration was carried out at the same time, from which it gets its nickname of the « golden basilica ».

The columns, capitals and parapets are all elements of high artistic value that witness the cleverness and taste of the Byzantine marble workers who laboured over a period of time that lasted from the II to the XII centuries. The rich paving of varied geometrical designs and representations of animals is a very beautiful example of marble mosaic art carried out in the XII century. In the centre, in front of the iconstasis, is the great square of veined Greek marble which in the past the Venetians called the « sea » because of its wavering surface.

31

THE MOSAICS OF THE BASILICA. -

The wonder and suggestion that is shown when admiring the interior of the basilica is almost exclusively owed to the immense mosaic cycle that runs along the walls, the vaults and over the domes, and which covers a surface of more than forty thousand square metres. The start of this phantasmagoric mosaic cycle took place in the XI century in the time of Doge Domenico Selvo who governed the Republic from 1071 to 1084, and this was succeeded by a second phase which extended from the XII century to the XIII century.

The very rich and passionate Byzantine mosaic work found a thick and prodigious group of artists and technicians in Venice constituting a flowering Venetian School from the XI century onwards; this had taken up the moviment following Ravenna's example. After a period of refinement, the Venetian School assumed a real artistic physionomia whose fruits were seen in the XII and XIII centuries under the pressing of Romanesque architecture. An ulterior progress came about in the XIV century when mosaic decoration was inspired by Venetian pictorial traditions.

An early decline in the art of mosaic took place during the Renaissance, so much indeed that the Attorneys of the Republic called Paolo Uccello and Andrea del Castagno from Florence to strengthen it. In this way the passion of the Venetian mosaicists was renewed, and in the sixteenth centuries they worked from the cartoons of the greatest artists of the time: Titian, Lorenzo Lotto, Tintoretto, Veronese, Piazzetta, Salviati and Bassano etc.

We present you with a series of very beautiful details of the magnificent mosaics of the basilica owed to the workmen of the fourteenth century.

1) **Christ enthroned**
2) **The miracle of St. Mark**
3) **The Evangelist John**
4) **The Evangelist Luke**
5) **The Evangelist Mark**
6) **The Evangelist Matthew**
7) **Jesus in the garden**

DESCRIBVN · QVATUOR · ISTI
SCS IOH

L.HOSTIA TEPLO
L VSAT QS SACERDOS
MEO

QODNEQVENA TVRALITER NE N
SCS LVCA

FVIT SACE
DVS DIERDOS
EBISDNOME
ERO ZAHAS

NEC VT BINO: FIGVRAS
SCS MARC·

5

SIC ACTVS CHRISTI
SCT MAEV

6

VPPLEX SVAT VRBA SOPOR AT ADQVOSMOX

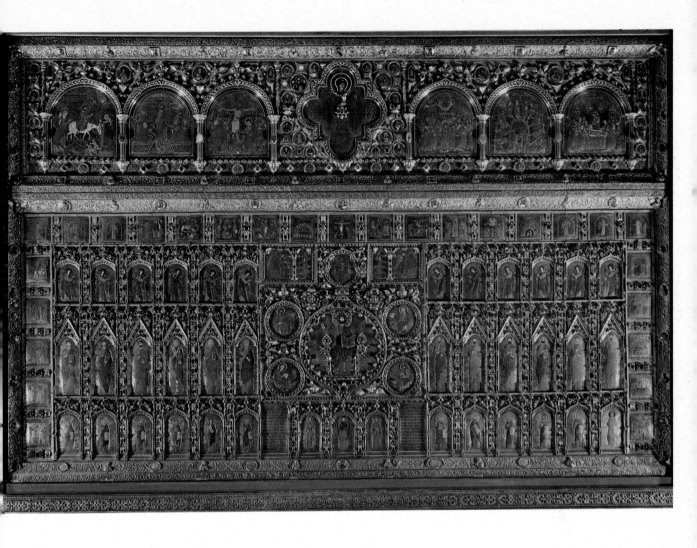

THE GOLDEN ALTARPIECE. - On the table of the main altar, under which is kept the body of St. Mark, stands a real masterpiece of mediaeval goldsmithery that goes by name of the **Golden Altarpiece.** Its primative formation came about in 978 when the Doge Pietro Orseolo gave the commission to the artists of Constantinople of realising it. However the Altarpiece was remade in 1105 and later enriched with gold and precious Byzantine enamels which come from the Monastery of Pantocrator in Constantinople and were brought to Venice during the Fourth Crusade in 1204.

Even if the material used has Eastern origins, the assemblage as a work of art was the fruit of the artistic sensibility of the Venetian goldsmith Giampaolo Boninsegna who carried it out in 1345. The wonderful composition is 3,40 metres wide by 1,40 metres high and is enriched with eighty enamels whose representations refer to episodes from the lives of the Redeemer, the Virgin and the Patron Saint, St. Mark. A miriad of diamonds, emeralds, rubies and topaz give relief to the Angels, Prophets, Evangelists and portraits of the Emperors of the East.

A detail of the mosaic in the dome over the baptismal font: **an apostle in the act of baptising.**

THE BAPTISTERY. - Here is a stupendous view of the Baptistery which has had its present form from 1350 at the wish of Doge Andrea Dandolo. In the middle is the great baptismal pool carried out by Tiziano Minio, Desiderio da Firenze and Francesco Segala (1545), the latter made the statue of St. John the Baptist which was cast in 1575. On the right is the tomb of Doge Andrea Dandolo of Venetian Gothic art owed to a family of sculptors: the De Sanctis family of the fourteenth century.

The mosaic work on the walls, vaults and domes was carried out by Venetian workmen of the fourteenth century and portrays episodes from the life of St. John the Baptist and the infancy of Jesus. On the end wall is the great « Crucifixion » with the portrait of Andrea Dandolo, in the dome above the baptismal font is « Christ invites the apostles to preach the glad tidings » and below all around is the « Apostles in the act of baptising people from various countries ». In the pendatives are four Doctors of the Greek Church. The Dome above the altar bears the mosaic of « Christ in glory » and in the pendatives are the figures of four Doctors of the Latin Church.

THE DUCAL PALACE

The powerful and fantastic palace, known as the Ducal Palace because from the IX century onwards the supreme head of the State lived here, was started in the time of Doges Angelo and Giustiniano Partecipazio in Byzantine style and founded on the Roman walls that previously stood there. This primative building was destroyed by a fire and reconstructed many times, but it was only in 1340 that it assumed its present structure, a structure that is the expression of the period in which Gothic art triumphed. The architect is unknown, but having been built in that time, the construction can be attributed to the stone cutter Filippo Calendario, one Pietro Baseio « magister porthus Palacii novi » and Proto Enrico. Anyway, the facade onto the pier and the one onto the Piazzetta were brought to a conclusion between 1400 and 1424.

The Ducal Palace: here is **the luminous facade** that overlooks the pier with the wonderful balcony in flowered Gothic style which was constructed in 1404 by Jacobello and Pier Paolo Dalle Masegne. It underwent alterations in 1575 and the addition of the statue of « Justice » by Alessandro Vittoria. The facade on this side is 71,50 metres long. In the foreground is the **Bridge of the Paglia** (Straw) that crosses the **Rio di Palazzo** onto which faces the third facade, the work of the architect Antonio Rizzo (1430-98).

The Ducal Palace: **the courtyard.** In the middle are the « puteals » in bronze; the first was sculpted by Niccolò dei Conti (1556), and the second by Alfonso Alberghetti (1559). On the right is the great facade in Gothic style in the lower part and Renaissance in the upper part, the architectural masterpiece of Antonio Rizzo (1483-98). On the left at the end is the facade of the Clock in baroque style, the work of the architect Bartolomeo Manopola (1614); on the right is the side of the Arch of the Foscari with the statue of F. Maria Primo della Rovere by the Florentine sculptor G. Bandini.

The Ducal Palace: **the porta della Carta** (the door of paper) so-called because clerks waited here to compile documents to be presented in the various offices of the Republic. The precious decoration in flowered Gothic taste was carried out by Giovanni and Bartolomeo Bon in 1438. The figures of « Virtues » are of particular beauty and can be seen in the niches of the pilasters. In the tondo above the three lighted windows is the bust of the Evangelist St. Mark and above it the statue of Justice. Over the portal is the « Doge Francesco Foscari and the winged lion » a sculpture by L. Ferrari (1885) which substitutes the one similar to it destroyed in 1797.

The Ducal Palace: **the Hall of the Council of Ten.** Here the much dreaded magistery assembled to investigate the cases for crimes of political nature against the security of the State. The pictorial cycle that decorates the room bears relation to the duties which were to inspire the conduct of the State. On the left wall is « Pope Alexander III, Barbarossa and Doge Ziani » by Francesco Leandro da Ponte; on the right wall is « The Adoration of the Magi » by Aliense. On the ceiling is « Jove crushing the Vices » an eighteenth century copy of a work by Veronese which can be found in the Louvre.

The Ducal Palace: **The Hall of the College** because here the College composed of the very high personalities of the Republic presided over by the Doge assembled. It dealt with the affairs of State and gave audiences to ambassadors. The architecture is owed to Palladio (1573). There are very beautiful pictorial masterpieces by Paolo Veronese on the ceiling, on the walls over the Tribune is the « Victory of Lepanto » also by Paolo Veronese, and on the right wall at the end is « The Mystical Wedding of St. Catherine » by Domenico Tintoretto, and the « Doge Niccolò da Ponte invoking the Virgin » by Jacopo Tintoretto.

The Ducal Palace: **The Hall of the Major Council.** Here the reunions of the greater Venetian magistery were held which organised the management of the State. We show a general view because the room is 54 metres long, 25 metres wide and 15,40 metres high. Destroyed by the fire in 1577 it was reconstructed as it is today by Antonio da Ponte and decorated with subjects suggested by the Florentine erudite Girolamo de' Bardi and by the Venetian historian F. Sansovino. The pictorial decoration is inspired by the celebration of the glories of the Republic. Above the Tribune is the grandiose canvas by Tintoretto of « Paradise », and on the ceiling in the large rectangle is the « Venice between the gods receives the homage of the subjected people » by Jacopo Tintoretto.

The Ducal Palace: **the Hall of Scrutiny.** Girolamo de' Bardi suggested the subjects also in this room for the pictorial decoration on the ceiling and walls that exalts the seafaring glories of the Republic; the room was reconstructed by Antonio da Ponte after the fire in 1577. At the end of the room is the Triumphal Arch built by A. Tirali in 1694 in honour of Doge Francesco Morosini after the conquest of the Peloponnese. On the right wall is the « Battle of Lepanto » by A. Vicentino; and after the door is « The Victory of the Dardanelles » by Pietro Liberi.

LOOKING AROUND VENICE

The gondolas slip silently and lightly along the picturesque Rio di Palazzo which flows into the pier flowing alongside the Ducal Palace.

THE BRIDGE OF SIGHS. - This is a dainty suspended bridge that crosses the Rio di Palazzo, in baroque style it is owed to the architect Antonio Contino (1599), and unites the Ducal Palace with that of the Prisons. The prisoners that were to appear before the court passed over this bridge, it was their only chance to see the Lagoon from the three lighted windows and to sigh for their lost liberty.

In the Dorsoduro section is the **Church of San Barnaba** built in 1749 thanks to the work of Lorenzo Boschetti. The facade is· a classical type of the Corinthian order with a tympanum. One notes the fine bell tower in Romanesque style.

In the Castello section is the very lovely **church of San Zaccaria** which opens on to the little square of the same name. The temple was built in the X century, but afterwards reconstructed between 1470 and 1500 by ςhe architects Antonio Gambello and Mauro Codussi, giving it its magnificent facade in six levels, a real masterpiece of Venetian Renaissance architecture. Over the portal is the statue of St. Zaccariah by Alessandro Vittoria, and below, at the sides in Renaissance frames are figures of the Prophets.

Rio San Moisé passes in front of the church of the same name and flows into the Grand Canal between Palazzo Tiepolo and Palazzo Treves dei Bonfili.

The Church of San Moisé which has been in existence from the VIII century in honour of St. Victor, seems to have been reconstructed in X century by one Moisé Venier who gave it the name of his particular patron Saint.

In the Castello section, one can find Campo **Santa Maria Formosa** which is rich with famous and artistic buildings, among them the church of the same name.

One of the many charact-
eristic and picturesque Venetian canals which wind their
way into the most far re-
moved parts of the city.

In the monumental **Campo San Giovanni
and Paolo** in the Castello section, the eques-
trian statue of the condottiere **Bartolomeo
Colleoni** stands with the air of a conque-
ror. It is the masterpiece of the Florentine
sculptor Andrea del Verrocchio.

The Domenican church of **San Giovanni
and Paolo** is a fine example of Venetian
Gothic architecture, started in 1246 and
finished in 1430. It is the Pantheon of Venetian glories because here rest the tombs of
those who really deserved the recognition
of the « Serenissima ».

The incomparable and impressive **interior of Santa Maria Gloriosa dei Frari.** Twelve pillars with wooden chains divide the space into three naves with a roof of pointed arch vaults. In the centre is the Choir with very beautiful sculptures by the Bon and Lombardo families.

SANTA MARIA GLORIOSA DEI FRARI. - This can be found at the Ca' Grande in the section of San Polo. The church, which constitutes the most important architectural building in Venetian Gothic style after St. Marks, was built for the Order of Minor Friars of St. Francis between 1340 and 1443. It seems that its architect was Fra Scipione Bon. Like San Giovanni and Paolo, it contains the tombs of illustrious personages of the Republic and numerous masterpieces of art. The austere and imposing facade divided by pilasters and columns, bears « Christ blessing » by A. Vittoria and the « Madonna and St. Francis » by B. Bon over the door.

Near to Campo San Trovaso (S. Gervasio and Protasio) in the Dorsoduro section, and on the canal of the same name, is this picturesque view of a « squero », that is, a boatyard for the construction and repair of gondolas. Venice had many such boatyards, and the one that one sees here is an example of how the old houses of the ordinary people must have been built in wood and brickwork. Behind it is the church of San Trovaso, in existence from the XI century and reconstructed in Palladian style in 1584.

The curious Lombard style **winding staircase** that one can admire in the adjacent courtyard of Palazzo Contarini Dal Bovolo. It is the work of Giovanni Candi who carried it out in 1500.

THE ISLAND OF MURANO: Originally it was called Amuriam and it constitutes one of the largest islands of the Venetian lagoon. Like Venice this also is formed by various little islands intersected by canals with bridges, foundations and alleys. It was perhaps formed in the X century, and was selfgoverning; it had the right of its own nobility and the priviledge of coining the so-called « oselle » or commemoration money for the election of the Doge of Venice. It prospered well because of its numerous industries and the particular disposition of the Serenissima.

Murano is famous for its glass masters. **The art of glass blowing,** started in 1289, became very developed in the fifteenth and sixteenth centuries, was made more precious by new techniques in the eighteenth century, and declined in the last century; today it has returned to its former splendour with an artisan production of high artistic level. In the photograph is a phase in the working of the glass.

The apse of the basilica of **Santa Maria and Donato** in Venetian-Byzantine style of the XII century.

In the photograph: a picturesque view of the island so dear to painters for the changeability of its colouristic tonality.

THE ISLAND OF BURANO: Its foundation is owed to the inhabitants of Altino who escaped from the invasion of Attila, and it keeps a characteristic feeling from its distant past in its dialect which really seems to come from the primative Altino pronunciation. The sixteenth century parish church of San Martino is interesting with a vaulted ceiling and in a Latin cross divided into three naves; among its diverse works of art it contains a grandiose « Crucifixion », by Giambattista Tiepolo carried out in around 1725. The great musician Baldassarre Galluppi known as Buranello was born in Burano (1703-85).

THE LACE MAKING OF BURANO: the ancient island is even more famous for its exquisite and artistic « merletti » (pillow lace), and industry which gave it an enviable economic prosperity, especially as this manufacture was completely carried out on needles, and because of its lightness and variety of stitches has conquered the preference of women of every nationality.

61

THE ISLAND OF TORCELLO: On the left the most important monument on the island, the **Cathedral of Santa Maria Assunta;** on the right the beautiful Church of Santa Fosca. The byzantine style cathedral was founded in 639, but underwent modifications in 864 and 1008. The construction of the imposing bell tower dates back to the eleventh century. The interior of the cathedral has a basilical plan, and is divided into three naves. On the walls of the entrance is a grandiose and beautiful mosaic of the twelfth century depicting the "Universal Judgement." The mosaic decoration which continues along the walls represents other subjects. The **Church of Santa Fosca,** in the style of Ravenna, was rebuilt in the eleventh century. The exterior has an harmonious arcade supported by white marble columns, and a pentagonal apse. The interior, in the form of a Greek cross, is transformed from a square form to a circular one because of the program to eventually add a dome which was never executed. The entire church is very interesting from the architectural point of view.

FLOODS IN VENICE – *The phenomenon of high tides (called "acqua alta" or high waters in Venetian) is such a common experience that the Venetians have come to accept them philosophically, without any big fuss. The water seems to have a special fondness for Piazza San Marco end the Basilica, wh re it can get more than 1½ feet deep so that it is possible to see a gondola on the square, or even beneath the arcades. In the photo, the improvised wooden platform set up for pedestrian traffic is clearly visible in the middleground.*

INDEX